What Would a Person Do?
Thoughts on Directing and Living

By Kimberly Senior

For Martha.

INTRODUCTION

We encounter a moment in rehearsal where an actor is faced with the challenge: I have this cup of coffee in my hand, but I also want to hug this person. Stumped by this obstacle, the actor turns to me for guidance. I look at this brilliant actor, who I love dearly, and simply ask "What would a person do?" And at that moment, the title of this book was born. Acting is hard- and that's not facetious. An actor has to say words, in the right order, written by someone else. Put intention behind them. Be nimble enough to change those intentions at any second based on what they receive from a scene partner. Plumb the rich emotional depths of themselves. Draw from their personal lives, exposing their demons. Become experts in other professions, other cultures, other relationships they haven't experienced. And while they're doing all that, they have to wear clothes designed and selected by someone else and act like it's the most normal thing in the world. They're under artificial lights, on a set, holding objects and walking through doors pretending it's just any old day ending in Y! And did I mention they're being WATCHED! Critiqued, admired, challenged, and adored by an audience ranging from 12-1200 each night, often eight shows a week!

This collection of tiny "thoughts" is drawn from my experiences in making and teaching theater where the question "What would a person do?' is a constant refrain which has led me to write a book that is not exclusively for theater makers but also for those complex humans who we so often study. My true passion lies in human behavior and all of my work is an exploration of that.

—

Human behavior when falling in love, human behavior when enduring war. Attempting to understand why good people sometimes do bad things and also understanding the spark that ignites when someone ordinary rises to the extraordinary. How it feels to bask in the glow of someone who truly sees you and how it feels to be utterly alone, even in a room full of people. This unrelenting curiosity has driven me through directing over 200 professional productions across American stages and driven my curriculum over 30 semesters of teaching at the university, graduate, and professional training levels. It has guided me through two marriages, even more great loves, raising two children, navigating friendships, professional relationships, and family. It has carried me through grief and heartbreaks and has pushed me to rebuild again and again.

This book is inspired by the students and collaborators who laughed at my jokes, repeated my phrases, shared them with others. Let this book serve as a reminder that there's always a larger context and a broader perspective. Instead of getting hung up in the micro wins and losses of our lives we can simplify when we pull back the lens. I came up with a vocabulary unintentionally. I thought everyone used the words, phrases, and ideas that I did. I didn't follow a typical path. I've never been to graduate school, assisted anyone, or had a fellowship. I've never gotten a grant and have no famous relatives nurturing me since childhood and taking me under their wings. I didn't graduate from a conservatory program. I didn't pursue my career in the city where I grew up or went to college. I've never waited tables or nannied. I followed a different path than many others. I offer here my findings from the 25+ years I've

spent observing and living my one human, wild and precious life.
(Thanks, Mary Oliver.)

HOW TO READ: This book is for everyone. This book is inspired by
Sarah Ruhl's *100 Essays I Don't Have Time to Write: On Umbrellas and Sword
Fights, Parades and Dogs, Fire Alarms, Children and Theater* which reinforced
for me that brevity is not only the soul but also the spark of wit. It is also
inspired by *The Pocket Pema Chödron,* a little yellow book I have taken
around the world and sought both solace and inspiration from.

I think it might mean one thing to an actor and another to a designer. I
think it might be meaningful to both fathers and daughters. A lawyer
might glean some new insight from here as much as a biochemist. It is
meant to be a quick look into understanding essential human behavior.
This book does not need to be digested cover to cover. It does not need
to be read in order. It is designed to be pop-up bits of inspiration and
insight. Open to any page!

AND: This is just the first edition. It's been nearly impossible to finish
because I consider everything a living document. So, while you're
reading this, I'm already adding and deleting and revising and responding
to the world around me.

Table of Contents

Foreword
By Marti Lyons

I first had the pleasure of working with Kimberly Senior when I assisted her on THE PILLOWMAN at Redtwist Theatre in 2010. I had just finished working with another director who was notorious for making assistants cry, and I was no exception. I remember my nerves on the first day of rehearsal at Redtwist's storefront space on Bryn Mawr as Kimberly was already legendary in Chicago and I wanted very much to impress her. I remember sitting around a folding table in the lobby of the small storefront space and how Kimberly launched the rehearsal by dazzling the room with her insights into the text and vision for the production. And I remember how after the first read-through, when the company was discussing the play, Kimberly invited my thoughts on the material and immediately established that I was her valued collaborator.

Throughout that process, I observed closely as Kimberly directed the show with precision and curiosity; diligence and humor; passion and elegance. In rehearsal, Kimberly would share a profound insight, crack a joke, and then remind an actor to simply do what a person would do. Then, on our breaks, she would head out to the lobby to meet her babysitter and her two children who would stop by each day so that she could spend time with them. I was captivated by Kimberly's brilliance, her humanity, and her joie de vivre. She was masterful at her craft but also so much FUN as a person. During rehearsals she cut to the heart of the play, all while winning the hearts of her collaborators.

And even in the chaos of making such a challenging piece in such a short amount of time while raising two small children, Kimberly always had time to connect with me. She encouraged my ideas, comments, and collaboration. She challenged my thinking while building my confidence. Because this is Kimberly; a director with a fierce, unfaltering artistry who somehow never misses an opportunity to build up her mentees, collaborators, family and friends.

THE PILLOWMAN was one of (twelve??? How many was it??) hit productions that Kimberly directed that year. It was just one of many notable seasons that Kimberly has had before and since, and but one of our many, many collaborations. But for me, it was a formative experience. The lessons I gleaned from that process have been foundational to my directorial process. And I cannot help but note, writing this with my infant daughter asleep on my chest, how my time with Kimberly has also impacted my life. She is a person I have quoted in rehearsal rooms, classrooms, and in daily life for the last fifteen years. She is someone I look to and turn to when the going gets tough. And I am not the only one. Kimberly is a luminary artist and a remarkable human being. Her legacy is already being cultivated by an army of mentees who pass her knowledge down person to person and process to process. I could not be more thrilled that she has documented her experience and is sharing it with the world so that others will benefit from her wisdom, as so many of us have.

I remember Kimberly once saying that what makes each artist unique is how their own experience meets the material they encounter; that what is obvious to one person is opaque to the next and that this is what each artist can bring to their craft. And, indeed, part of Kimberly's particular genius is her ability to elicit the profound through the practical. What would a person do? It is such an obvious question. But, as you will discover, what is obvious to Kimberly illuminates the world for the rest of us.

THOUGHTS ON DIRECTING

360 Degrees

We can't make art in a vacuum.

When I was applying to colleges my parents forbade me from going to a Conservatory even though I knew I was destined to be a Big Broadway Star, triple threat that I was. The logic was if I wanted to be an actor, didn't I need to learn about the world? Weren't history and sociology classes even more vital than Laban and yoga? I grumbled at the time and ultimately ended up with a BA in Theater from Connecticut College and couldn't be happier about it.

My parents' advice I dispense constantly. If you want more specific technique regarding theatre training you can go to grad school. Or teach yourself by surrounding yourself with geniuses, working constantly, buying more books than you can afford and saying YES (which was my route.) What I learned in Anthropology and Sociology I reference far more often than my Ibsen Scene Study class.

I now refer to this as 360 Degree Learning or 360 Degree Artistry. We should be drawing from all the amazing resources in this gorgeous world. The worlds we put on stage are rarely populated with artists! We're insufferable, who would make art about us? Instead, our work is populated with union laborers, corporate lawyers, unhoused mothers, and corrupt intelligence officers to name a few. We traffic in fractured families, unjust systems of oppression, and complex identities. These subjects reside in the world, not in textbooks, and certainly not in theater classrooms.

It is incumbent upon us to travel. To feel foreign, to make our way through discomfort. We must talk to people outside our tiny bubble. We must notice and pay attention on transportation. I promise you, you don't need to doomscroll social media on the subway. Look up.

I'm a big walker. One year (2014) I endeavored to only walk when on the island of Manhattan. No public transportation, no cabs, even in inclement weather. It was part of my 360 Degree Learning. (Although I've learned a lot from Uber drivers over the years.) It really changed how I planned my days, knowing that my on-foot commute was going to take some time. I talked on the phone a lot more. But the most significant is what I noticed. Guys on street corners dispensing advice to their overseas relatives on flip phones. Women (being ignored) with strollers. Tiny deals and negotiations everywhere. Even tinier intimacies- a held hand on a street corner, the careful way a mother protects her daughter. So many stories.

These are the stories that populate our work. Be curious, pay attention, bring these stories into your rehearsal rooms, your offices, your life. You will begin to notice a marriage of your personal and professional self. A holistic way of walking through the world. Read books, magazines. Listen to podcasts. Go to museums. Bring these resources into your work, too. Using the world around us as research and inspiration further animates and textures our work and helps connect us to one another.

Defying What Your Teachers Taught You

Painting something black doesn't render it invisible.

Our theater, at its very best, is current (or even in advance of our culture). It demands our process remain relevant. Changing technologies have reimagined theatrical design. I remember when sound design meant pressing your tape recorder achingly close to the radio speaker hoping they played that one fantastic song that must end your play on the radio and equally hoping your little brother didn't come barreling through your bedroom, naked, with a football tucked underneath his armpit. True story.

We don't have to slay our heroes to remain current. There are fundamentals, foundations, that will remain true no matter the era. One of my closest collaborators, scenic designer Jack Magaw, always says "You can't deconstruct the kitchen until you understand how to build the kitchen." I can't believe how often I still refer to my Aristotle or how I rely on David Ball's *Backwards and Forwards* when I can't figure out a scene. But we must keep pace with changing technologies, changing symbols, changing conversations, and, ultimately, understand our audience demands and deserves our fresh eye.

What we were taught in 1970, 1983, 1995, 2002, 2013…all of this must constantly be re-examined and re-thought and on occasion we will return to the original for why reinvent the wheel… it is the *examination* that is our imperative.

I'm using the word "teacher" here in a global sense. Sure, it's your Text Analysis teacher from 2008 but it's also the plays that inspired you, mentors, people you assisted, bosses.

The less obvious is how our process has changed in the art and craft of less tangible storytelling. We must use the world around us to source our work. That world is ever changing- social mores, political spheres, language usage. Discussion of gender binaries, the advent of the internet and social media, Black Lives Matter and #MeToo. And so much more. Our world is a living organism. We must demand the same of our process.

Using relied upon conventions of staging and design no longer work because they have become tired to our eyes. They no longer awaken surprise, or present to us our world through a new lens. Many of us were taught proscenium staging gestures. Our theaters today often offer a different relationship to an audience. Having full frontal access to an actor in a theater in the round is impossible for all audience members all of the time. Let's feel less obligated to "cheat out" and compelled to find a staging that best serves the moment. Maybe where you are sitting in the theater offers you a different perspective than another audience member. And then you can discuss that after, challenge one another with your different perspectives. It's become an obsession of mine, placing an actor with their back to the audience in the first ten minutes of a play. We feel in the audience like a fly on the wall, forced to imagine the look on a face- I am trusting that what remains hidden is as interesting as what is seen.

—

15

Similarly, we must examine our intentions in a moment. An affirming squeeze on the shoulder from professor to student means something different to a modern audience than it did fifty years ago. David Mamet's *Oleanna* helped redefine that as did the multitude of sexual abuse scandals arising daily from our university system.

Here are some examples of what I am learning to do without- even though these seemed quite reasonable solutions, or shortcuts, for some time:

- Painting something black doesn't make it disappear. Instead, let's see what happens if we light it up, let it shine!

- "Suspension of disbelief" means something different as time passes. There's a contract with the audience, of course. We know it's not "real". But what we ask of them is ever changing. Suspend your disbelief in a more literal theater of the 1950s was believing an apartment was on the third floor even when you didn't see the whole environment. We're less rigorous about reality now so what is it that you need the audience to buy into for the storytelling to be successful?

- Playing loud music in a transition rarely obscures actors or crew bumping into furniture in the dark. What if we worked with our designers and humans doing the change and create something elegant and interesting to look at?

- Blue doesn't always mean night, red doesn't always mean violence. You knew that, but just in case. Nor must the future be metallic. Or the past sepia.

- A list of important phone numbers on a fridge in a kitchen doesn't universally mean "human beings live here." Especially since all of our important numbers are now stored in our phones. Pay attention to the human details. Our audiences are too smart for blanketed gestures.

Chekhov's Dope

All plays are contemporary. The end.

In fact, so many plays we see as dusty old classics were written by the most progressive thinkers of the time. Imagine a world in which plays taught people how to live! We must not forget this is such an ancient tradition. And in every culture the virtue of storytelling brought communities together where they were able to work out the most challenging parts of their existence. Plays, and their issues, were cutting edge.

Writers, in their time, were often counterculture. We have done a serious disservice to history when we think of them as dusty old classics. Sure, Chekhov was a white dude. But he wasn't old. And he was also saving lives as a volunteer doctor. And building hospitals. And trying to destroy a really fucked up hierarchical culture. I *hated* Chekhov in college. How could Sonya love Astrov for EIGHT YEARS and not say a word about it? To anyone?! I couldn't love someone for eight minutes and not shout it from the rooftops. I felt totally alienated by the world of the play. The 1890s in Russia and the 1990s in Connecticut had very little in common as far as I was concerned.
And then I met Curt Columbus and he was translating all of Chekhov's plays. He opened my eyes to the fact that these plays are actually written in quite colloquial vernacular. He was writing translations that were act-able. The people in those plays want to fuck people they shouldn't.

They dream big and don't know how to achieve those dreams. They are just like us! Curt opened my eyes to how we were getting it all wrong. Instead of being stuck on the mechanics of a samovar we should be examining the mechanics of the human heart.

What if you were to perceive *Hedda Gabler* as a world premiere every night? It's the only time that *this* audience, in *this* theatre, on *this* day, with *this* group of artists will come together. We must embrace this notion because it is one of the few things that only the live theatre can do.

Size Matters

A lot of theaters have a "small" theatre and a "big" theatre. Traditionally the "big" theatre holds *A Christmas Carol* and *All My Sons* and other plays by and about white men. And the smaller stages are for the other 69% of the population. Theatres tend to put plays on their bigger stages that they predict will have bigger ticket sales.

I wish we were spending more time programming plays for their scale. What size space wants to hold this story? Or are the two in contrast. I remember seeing Bob Falls' stunning production of John Logan's *Red* on the Albert Stage, which has over 800 seats. It's a two-hander, in an artist's loft. One might think these two guys want to be contained in the smaller theatre- but the Albert served the play perfectly. The vastness of the space illuminated their attempts to communicate and find each other over great distance. I left the play thinking about how small I felt in the world.

The near opposite of that is my production of *The Diary of Anne Frank.* Thirteen actors crowded into the space the size of my living room. As those families were while hidden in the attic. Only fifty people could see the play at a time, and they were also in cramped quarters.

None of this to say is that plays must be confined to a certain scale. It's important to *consider* scale and configuration in your concepts, your design, in your audience's experience from the street to the seat.

In a 99-seat theatre we can better appreciate the raise of an eyebrow, the nervous tic of a bouncing knee. And in a 990-seat theatre, we can better encounter the howl of grief and the enormity of oppression.

I want to add here that the size of the theatre, the number of seats, the cost of the tickets, the size of your paycheck… none of these things affect the scale of the work, and the scale of your heart. It is equally thrilling and important to open a play above a Mexican restaurant as it is on Broadway.

Playwrights Know What's Up

Don't fuck up a playwright's play.

They give you all the information you need to do your job. Why waste time in a rehearsal room thinking of all the scenes the playwright didn't write? They don't want those scenes in the play, otherwise they would've written them. The questions in the rehearsal should not be around what isn't there but rather what *is*. Those are the scenes the playwright chose to include for very specific reason. It's our task to understand why and further illuminate that for our audiences. Why diagnose or solve mysteries the playwright has intentionally left mysterious? If the playwright doesn't give you a character's profession, for example, then that is not relevant for the telling of *this* particular narrative. What can you glean from what you are given?

Theresa Rebeck is a wonderful example of a playwright that doesn't give explicit stage directions. For example, from her play *Mauritius*:

"A shop. JACKIE stands in light, holding a book. PHILIP at the counter, reading a book. There is someone in the corner of the room, reading a newspaper."

We know it's a shop. We know there's a book. We know we need a counter, a corner of the room, a newspaper. We must read further to see what this shop requires. The answers will be found inside of the scenes. Also note that her characters have names and what they are doing but little other information is given. Yet her work includes incredibly complex character *behavior*. Work from there.

By contrast, you could look at the opening stage directions in William Inge's *Come Back, Little Sheba.*

"It is the downstairs of an old house in one of those semi-respectable neighborhoods in a Midwestern city."

Already I have so much information! Already I can ask so many questions (of which the playwright may reveal to me answers later…) The house is old. How long have they lived there? Semi-respectable: hmmm, do the current inhabitants lean to the semi- or the -respectable side? A Midwestern city. Doesn't matter which one.

Further on:

"In such areas, houses are so close together, they hide each other from the sunlight."

I love this part. Inge tells us so much. We get an awareness of the outside world, that privacy might be hard to come by. In fact, the act of other houses harming the actual growth of one another is wonderful to note. When we meet neighbors, we know how close they are to us.

Instead of creating answers, look for the questions. Allow for the possibilities. When you attempt to "fill in the blanks", you are ultimately playwriting for the playwright. They don't need you to do that. They are very good at their jobs. Let their work ignite your imagination towards their story. Trust that you have everything you need. There is something very Zen about accepting what is there and just making that.

Finding the Bones

Assuming makes an *ass* out of *u* and *me*.

When we first meet someone--be it in real life or a character we encounter in a play--we are very excited to get to know them. So excited that we might rush to conclusions instead of allowing them to unfold for us. How do we avoid assumptions and begin a substantial learning process? We can identify the _bones_.

What is true about a play no matter what? What are the things the playwright gives you, so you don't have to act them? Bones are familial relationships. Occupations. Pieces of personal history. They are true about the characters no matter who plays the role. These facts provide the skeleton.

I have a sister named Katie. I don't walk around with her acting all "sisterly"--I mean what does that even mean? There are so many ways to be a sister. The bones are often broad strokes, where what we really seek are the details that make our characters, and our human selves, so specific. Katie is my sister. It's a *bone*, it's true no matter what. And when I tell you, my audience, that she's my sister, I don't have to act that or demonstrate that in any way because you trust me. These are undeniable-in-a-court-of-law things.

Some of the bones in Lynn Nottage's *Sweat*:

- Jason is Tracy's son
- Tracy, Cynthia, Jason, and Chris all work at Olstead's

- Stan used to work at Olstead's until he got injured; now he tends the bar

- Oscar was born in Pennsylvania

And so on. What happens when you come up against something like Jessie calling Tracy "bossy" in *Sweat*? Is that a bone? Nope. It's *bias*. It requires further investigation. In the same way we don't have to do anything about acting out things that are true about us no matter what, we need to examine what and why others say about us what they do. Why does Jessie call Tracy bossy? Would other characters say the same? The actor playing Tracy can't just act "bossy." And what does that look like anyway? Every character is entitled to their own opinion of every other character. Your mother would describe you differently than your lover or your child would.

This behavior is a type of code-switching (which is often supported with our diction and syntax in these situations). This basic approach to character is a wonderful place to start in a rehearsal room. It's also a wonderful exercise in our own self-knowledge. I discovered this in the classroom. I do not need to *act* like the teacher. I *am* the teacher.

That's a bone. I wasted some early months teaching by attempting to be teacherly--therefore wasting time I could've spent reaching my students, exploring curricular challenges, and, mostly, connecting honestly with my students.

Another example of this are moments when I check myself almost exaggerating what a terrific mother I am.

I carry an insecurity with me about the way others perceive me as a mother since I work so often, and so often am away from home. When I remember Mother is one of my bones, I am able to soften in the role. Knowing that seeing my children in relationship to me, and to the world around them, says everything about that role.

On The Big Picture

In rehearsal, we run the play every day. There is a method to my madness.

I talk a lot about MACRO and MICRO thinking. MACRO to me means the whole play. In life terms, that's your whole life. MICRO is the juicy details, the texture in moments, the careful calibration of intention moment to moment. Both in plays and life. You can't have one without the other.

When we go to the gym- lift weights, running, biking- we use our big muscle groups- our lats, our glutes, our quads. That's macro work. It's an appearance of strength, it's how our bodies appear to be built. And sometimes, even if we think it's boring and repetitive, we have to go to Pilates and work those smaller muscles, those teensy muscles that connect the hamstring to the glutes and are doing some really important work.

In process I will quickly stage the play so we can see the big picture. You have to get to the end to understand the beginning. Never is this more important than in tech. How often have you spent the whole first day on opening moments? What happens if you kind of skip through that and use it as vocabulary and vibe developing? By the time you get to the end of the play there's a whole new thing in the room. Now look at the beginning. Your time will be more productive, and the work will be way better.

Therefore, we run the play every day. We make a sketch and then keep revisiting it to fill in the details. When actor Hari Dhillon, who played Amir in *Disgraced* on Broadway, heard I wanted to run the play every day he was not happy. Why, he demanded to know. I talked him through my micro and macro thinking and we came up with the idea of having a target for every run. Instead of trying to make the play better every day, we would attempt to uncover myriad aspects of the work. I call this *orbiting*. We are circling around the play, the pillar of our storytelling and in so doing making new discoveries all the time. It removes a hierarchical structure to our process.

The target will teach us. I give targets based on what we need to discover. Is the play feeling too dark and weighted down? Let's use the target of "finding the humor" in the play. Play lacks dynamism? How about if all the actors are the best attorney for their character? And so on. After each run, I sit with the actors and we note where the target made sense and was useful- and where it wasn't. With these targets you make a lot of messes. These messes are so useful and remove the hierarchical structure from a rehearsal process. Time takes on different meaning. For instance, mining the humor may present discoveries in certain moments, yet completely undermine others. The actor Patrick Sabongui described the experience as "taking what worked from (the) runs and storing the other layers away, because you never know on any given night, or in a given moment, if one of those layers may actually be that one perfectly fitting missing piece." We need to see the whole thing in order to bring magic to the details. If we get too focused on what is happening in a singular moment, we lose sight of the whole story.

Although we are all working together to build the play, it is truly the director's job to keep the big picture in mind. This work helps actors stay at work in the moment to moment and reminds directors to zoom out and see the impact of the whole. How many times have you watched a play and you're like wow cool those actors are in a moment that I am zero percent invited into, because they spent hours in rehearsal hashing out details (that they playwright didn't intend- see: *Not Fucking Up a Playwrights Play*) and it's not in service of the whole story? We must always keep the whole in mind.

I use macro and micro when I'm attempting to fix something, too. If there's a moment not working, what happens if you zoom out and look at the structure that contains that moment? Are all the building blocks in place? They are? OK, zoom in. Maybe we're glossing over specifics, skipping a detail. When I want to get super micro, I refer to Katie Mitchell's brilliant book *The Director's Craft*. There is no greater book in which to counter the micro and specific.

This macro/micro thinking also affects the way we give notes. I think of it like this: sometimes I'm noting a paragraph, a bigger idea. Sometimes a sentence, we're getting more refined. Sometimes a word… "I know this is granular but…" We need to live in all of the modes. And take this care with ourselves. Ever had your heart broken? Zoom out, babe. There's a larger story that you're in.

Unnecessary Roughness

I grew up in northern New Jersey. The streets are definitely not in a grid. One of the local favorite subjects is how to get from point A to point B. Some of my favorite childhood memories are of sitting in the backseat of my parents' car listening to them bicker about which way is faster, which way has fewer lights. But, also, which way is more picturesque. Where you can see the beautiful houses. Or the best holiday lights.

I feel this way about blocking. The ground plan is a map. And your actors need to figure out point A to point B. Sometimes they want to be efficient, avoid detours. Other times they'll want something picturesque.

I tend to start blocking rehearsals with the actors "bumping into furniture." Without my intervention I'm interested in what shapes they make, what distance and intimacy looks like, what are some natural places to rest, to sit, to accelerate. I also joke that a pass without my intervention in the early stages proves my necessity ☺ After they've gone through the scene, I ask them what they've noticed, what they liked.
I usually end up moving a piece of furniture or two. Sometimes I will remove furniture entirely. Actors tend to have furniture "magnets"- there is something in them that is compelled to lean up against furniture, hide behind it, seek refuge. Similarly, they love a wall, a pole, any upright architecture to hold them up. No audience wants to see an actor cling to a settee for dear life. If there are too many places to sit onstage it diffuses tension.

When there are fewer seats than actors, we create something dynamic. In staging the dinner party at the end of Act 1 of Anton Chekhov's *Three Sisters* (in a riveting translation by Curt Columbus) there are notoriously "Thirteen at table!" What if there are only 12 seats? Vershinin is an unexpected guest, after all. Someone always needs to be up, perhaps we're crowded and intimate at the table in a way that can be of interest, so many possibilities are opened up for makeshift seating and necessary blocking.

Speaking of "necessary" blocking, I have a habit of over-staging plays at first. What are all the possible ways we can move and the myriad ways we can motivate that? I find that once I am watching runs of the play, I'm seeing so much busy movement. I think it's vestigial from when we are learning the play and don't know how to trust it yet. Since I'm never one to resist a sports reference, I'll often throw my imaginary football flag "Unnecessary blocking" which should be penalized as "Unnecessary roughness." Manhandling the play with too much blocking is a sure sign of insecurity.

I'm not interested in pre-blocking anything. I'm not interested in making pretty stage pictures. Those will emerge. It's almost backwards that we tend to start with blocking when we have so little emotional information about the characters and stories.

In our lives we walk in patterns. From the bedside to the bathroom to the kitchen. Our patterns are determined by our needs. As the artists involved become more deeply ensconced in the storytelling the blocking will emerge. And then the director can step in, nudge an inch, recalibrate a degree, and make something beautiful.

Rimbombare

I think one of the most fun challenges as a theater director is determining point-of-view, which is something a camera does for you in other media.

In film and television, the director gets to control what an audience sees, where they look. We have no such luck in the theatre. Some of that is pretty cool- different audience members get different experiences, notice different things, which allows for multiple interpretations. When I directed Eleanor Burgess' *The Niceties*, a two-hander about who has the right to tell the story of America, audiences argued for hours afterwards about whose side they were on. The film version of that is bound to have more of the director's opinion involved.

We do have a couple of tools at our disposal to help control this lens. Solid partnership with your lighting designer is a great place to start. Identifying powerful positions on stage with your actors another. Knowing when someone or something moves, it draws attention.

Another method is more subtle. When actors don't break eye contact, we need to keep both of them in the frame. I don't know where I got this notion- did I make it up? - but I call that unbroken eye contact *rimbombare* which is an Italian word that translates to rumble or thunder. When one actor looks away the audience has to choose whose story to follow. A couple is breaking up. In real life, at least one of them looks away. What if they maintain eye contact on stage? We stay with the couple in that moment.

Getting Through Doors and Other Troubling Human Behavior

A rehearsal room can feel like the Wild West.

It's a liminal space where anything seems possible. In Lars Von Trier's movie *Dogville* he echoes the rehearsal room by taping out on the floor an entire town. Nicole Kidman's emotions are remarkably laid bare with no structure behind which to hide.

And that's how it is in rehearsal. The set is taped out, the furniture is often temporary, objects are stand ins for the real thing to be provided for once we move to the theatre. Actors are still in their scripts, figuring out how to walk and talk at the same time. They are breaking down things we do in daily life without thinking- how do I hold a pen, how do I walk through a door, how do I love someone- as someone else, so it's like a child learning to walk.

It requires kindness and patience to help actors through this stage. A simple threshold in a door is enough to throw an actor who is carefully calibrating their every move to align with their intentions. Although it may look completely natural, nothing about acting is. Everything has meaning when you put it on stage. Therefore, things that a person might do, like walk through a door, have to be re-learned in order to align with the larger stage picture in the director's mind and to make sense to the body and intention of the actor.

Nisi Sturgis is one of the most precise and emotionally available actors I have ever encountered. She played Emily in three of my productions of Ayad Akhtar's *Disgraced* and brought a depth and humanity to the role that moved me throughout our 7 months on the road together.

One thing that I love about Nisi's process is that she speaks out loud to what she is doing in order to get it into her body. Emily has a difficult table setting sequence to be done during an intellectually complex conversation. Nisi had to navigate her every move to not distract from the text- how did each of her physical moves add to the discussion? In rehearsal every time Nisi walked through a door she would say "clickity" as if her moves were a line in the text (although the origin of "clickity" was another actor who had annoyed Nisi! It came in handy in any event.) In real life we don't think passing through a doorway as an obstacle to conversation but onstage it might be. Nisi's heightened awareness of this, along with her saying "plates," "glasses" and "napkins" helped us build a dynamic scene with enormous awareness of both the storytelling and her scene partners.

Ultimately it is the goal to empower actors to behave naturally and to become fluent in their character, so they are no longer thinking through "how and when do I pick up this mug." Fluency is when we are no longer translating between the self and the character. Rehearsal is practicing the scales.

Whose Play Is It Anyway?

MY PLAY!

I ask an actor: Whose play is it?

Their answer should be: MY PLAY!

Even if we only see a character for one crucial scene- like Mrs. Muller in John Patrick Shanley's *Doubt*- doesn't mean they are only there to serve the play. That one scene is the only play Mrs. Muller knows, so that's the whole play, it's her play. And she should play it as such. I'm not suggesting that actor write a whole back story and lug it onto stage. I'm saying this is the size of Mrs. Muller's play and it's from her point-of-view. What she wants and what she's willing to do to achieve that. This is a version of "there are no small parts, only small actors." I like my version better.

Ten Minute Play

Similarly to it being MY PLAY each character walks on to stage with a ten-minute play in mind. They've got their script, they're ready to enter, say what they need to say, get what they want and get out. Unfortunately, when they enter the scene, they find out that their scene partner seems to have the wrong pages (alas, it's *their* ten-minute play.) This is extremely motivating, a great way to stay present and stay on task. If there's a moment in rehearsal when an actor isn't quite sure what's happening in the scene, you can revisit this ten-minute play idea. What did you come in the scene to do? What obstacles are in your way? How is it not going your way? So, the rest of the scene, and sometimes even play, is attempting to get the other people into the same script as yours, the one where you are the hero and get exactly what you need.

In Yasmina Reza's play << *ART* >> Serge has bought a painting and invited his friend Marc over to see it. Serge thinks this is the greatest painting of all time. His ten-minute play goes a little something like this: I've invited my oldest friend, Marc, over to see my painting which I know he will also love and appreciate because, after all, he is my oldest friend, so we love the same things. Naturally. Marc comes for the visit, to see his oldest friend, Serge, who he also values and admires. But then, the canvas is revealed. Both ten-minute plays are upset by this. Marc is practically repulsed by the painting which sets into motion the series of events that make up the play. Both men are trying to recognize their oldest friend, but their opinions of this painting have turned everything upside down. Using the ten-minute play idea both characters attempt to get back into *their* play… Serge wants Marc to love the painting as he does, and Marc wants his friend to align with his values.

Both the notions- MY PLAY and the TEN MINUTE PLAY- are very activating for actors in terms of identifying what they want in any given scene or moment and why they are there. These ideas also help to create necessary conflict and obstacles for scenes.

Comedy's Obstacles

I've spent so much of my career making "barn burner" plays, plays about identity and politics and feelings. But what I really want to do is make people laugh. I love when I get to employ my influences (Carol Burnett, Three Stooges, Chris Rock) and if you get me to say, "that's so *stupid*!" in the rehearsal room you've won the funny lottery.

I spend a lot of time thinking about what's funny and why. The essence of clown is I have a task I want to accomplish, it means a lot to me, and there are obstacles. The obstacles create the comedy. For instance, I want to be the best piano player in history. Because then I can win the heart of my lifelong desire. But I'm tone deaf. And don't have a piano. Can you imagine the actual laws and the laws of decorum and gravity I am willing to break to achieve my goal? Comedy ensues.

And, wow, do you have to be brilliant in order to be stupid! There is so much math involved in timing the perfect moment. Octavia Chavez-Richmond, in our recent production of *The 39 Steps,* found so much comedy in every moment. She plays about 50 different characters in the play, as "Clown 1," and he Chief Inspector Albright had me in stitches. The Chief Inspector enters the stage in a high stakes moment in the climax of the play, ready to apprehend the murder suspect. Octavia played those stakes and when her target disappears, Octavia, in total resignation utters "He's escaped." Nothing funnier than an opposite. And did I mention the Chief Inspector had a lisp?

The dynamic actor, Nikkole Salter, cracks me the fuck up. When I was directing Kirsten Greenidge's *Our Daughters Like Pillars* I could barely give Nikkole notes through my laughter. When I told her how hilarious I found her she said "I am not funny. It is my circumstances which are funny." Play the circumstances, not the comedy. Brilliant.

Fluency

We use the word *fluency* primarily to describe one's aptitude with learning a new language. When we are fluent there is a flow and efficiency with how you express your ideas. When you are not fluent there is a step of translation. I see a window, I say "window" in English and then I find the word "finestra" in Italian. When I am fluent, I see the window and simply say "finestra." This is how the relationship should be between actor and character. In the beginning of the process the character is a foreign language. By performance, the actor is fluent.

The marvelous actor Tim Hopper experiences stage fright. Even though he's been a professional actor for decades, teaches acting, is a member of the Steppenwolf Theatre ensemble, he wants to run away before curtain nightly. When I asked him how he does it, he told me that he only needs to say the first line and the rest of the play will happen. So, he practices that first line in the wings and steps on stage and lets the play fly. He can do this because he is fluent.

The only way to do that is meticulous preparation. I call that "learning to forget." We do that in a number of ways. One way is blocking (See *On Blocking*.) We create these traffic patterns and make these maps and stage managers take copious notes and we call it "blocking." However, once we're in performance, that blocking should be the way that character moves, motivated by what they want and need. The actor is no longer remembering blocking, they are moving with fluency through the space.

Another way is through intention. I like to use a transitive verb per line. I _____ you. I flatter you. I intimidate you. These can be flexible but are a good shorthand in rehearsal. In rehearsal, we can speak to these verbs. By the time we're in performance those verbs are part of our fluency.

Once we are fluent we free up space in our brains to simply *be*. To listen and respond. Be present in the moment.

Knowing When to Say What to Whom

First of all, how do you organize your notebook? Think about it. Or do you use a huge legal pad and scrawl? My friend, and fellow director, Oliver Butler, takes his notes on post its, puts them on paper, and as he goes through them, he tosses the post it. A heap of crumpled post-its must be very satisfying for him.

I organize my notebook with tiny checkboxes down the side. I leave room in the margin to write who the note is for and asterisk the ones that are for me. I put an x through the box when I've given the note. I like to be able to go back and see what I've written, even referring to it. It's fascinating to be able to track the journey of the play this way. I find in previews it's helpful to review those early notes.

I also don't give all my notes all at once. Everyone needs a process. Sometimes I can see something that we will want to amend later down the road. On average, I give about 3 of the 5 notes I write down, roughly 60%. Learning the nuance of reading the actor is a tough job. And every actor is their own ecosystem. I know actors who want all the notes and want to go home and process. Other actors just want to go again, right now. Other actors want to discuss each and every note. That's also a factor in how I give them.

Once in this lifetime, so far, I tried an experiment that I called Envelope Directing. It was during a production of Harold Pinter's *Old Times* at Strawdog Theater, a three-hander featuring Abigail Boucher, Michaela Petro, and John Henry Roberts.

Three members of the ensemble who knew each other intimately and I had worked with multiple times. Because the play dealt with memory and personal history and betrayal and love, each character had a very subjective view on the events. I never once gave notes to the entire company. Sometimes I literally put my notes in an envelope and handed them to an actor. Other times I did three notes sessions, all in private. At the closing performance the actors shared what they believed was true of the play. (Very few *bones*- see: *Finding the Bones*.) Much like scale, we can consider the way we give notes to suit the nature of the content. And the company.

Most importantly, notes, like a lot of dairy, can *expire*. Just because you said it Tuesday doesn't mean it's valid on Friday. Actors want to set in stone what you say. It gives them structure and boundaries which lead to confidence. Sometimes though, notes change. Our notes evolve as our relationship to the play evolves. So, we might have to say "I know on Tuesday I felt like you were fighting to be seen by him but today on Friday I see you're exposing his betrayal. It's a little shift, and it's definitely an expiration of Tuesday's note." Or even more simply "I know Tuesday I asked you to grab the tissue on that line but today on Friday I know it's better on the next one. Expire Tuesday, please."

Note Behind the Note

I've been using the same orange Rhodia notebook since I received my first one as a gift from my all-time favorite art partner, Ayad Akhtar, in 2011. It's spiral bound, soft yet sturdy, and bright bright orange. The night before 1st rehearsal for *Disgraced* on Broadway I had the heart stopping, is-this-my-life moment of chatting with Bartlett Sher, Cherry Jones, and Ayad under the night sky on the plaza at Lincoln Center. Cherry turns to Bart and says "Bart, do you have any advice for Kimberly as she heads into rehearsal for her first Broadway show?" Bart replied "Never carry a notebook. People will think you want their opinions."

But I do. I desperately want their opinions. But that's me. Think about it. Are you in a space where you're welcoming notes?

An important thing to remember: the note giver isn't as familiar with the work as you are. This is valuable because a) they can have the innocence of your audience and b) they might be wrong about the note. This is where The Note Behind The Note comes in. An Artistic Director tells you the end of act 1 fails to hit a proper climax. They're not necessarily *wrong-* but it's not the end of the act that's the problem. When you examine the situation, you find you failed to leave a crucial breadcrumb that would really ignite the end of the act.

When you receive notes, they aren't gospel. No matter who they are from. But they are all worth considering. Consider who gave the note, their perspective. It might not be the right time for you to hear it.

It might not be your version of the story. It might be a note about something else but they diagnosed it a moment too late.

The one totally awesome time I got to work with Judd Apatow was when I directed Chris Gethard's comedy special *Career Suicide*. When I was working with the postproduction team on the edit, Judd would get sent drafts along the way. One day, Judd called me and said, "The part about Burning Man- do you love it?"

"Yeah, Judd, I do."

"Well, ok."

"What? Tell me."

"No, if you love it, what do I know? You know the work so much better than me."

I, of course, revisited that section, trying to understand what he was getting at. And I did still love that section. And then I investigated a few moments prior. I realized that the setup for the story was what was incorrect. Thus, the note behind the note was born. Plus, serious props for Judd Apatow being a great note-giver and boss. I use "Do you love it?" all the time.

Hamlet's Suffering

Have you seen that show? *Hamlet?* And the actor playing the titular character bows so gravely, lets you know how arduously they've worked for the past three hours that your applause is sheer gratitude for their endurance? Let's not do that.

The curtain call is when you are no longer your character. The play is over. It is an opportunity for the audience to say, "Thank you" and for the actors to say "thank you" right back. There is no fourth wall. So, there is no need for hysterics, platitudes, poses or any other nonsense. It is human beings, sharing space. Saying thank you for sharing your gift (acting) and thank you for sharing your gift (receiving).

I also love a fun curtain call song so everyone knows the play is over. Using a pop song that feels adjacent is always a good call. Some examples:

Hedda Gabler; Amy Winehouse's *Back to Black*
Gina Gionfriddo's *Rapture, Blister, Burn*; Liz Phair's *6'1"*
Yasmina Reza's *<<ART>>*; Rolling Stones, *Paint It Black*

It is one of the rare opportunities in life to truly be in community. The audience, regardless of their size, has just gone through an experience together, watching your play.
They're likely to have a myriad of opinions and feelings but in this moment, the curtain call, is the purity of this first moment of coming to

consciousness after being lost in the world of the play. By the actors being simply actors and no longer characters it gives the audience the opportunity to bridge back into reality and truly share the space, and the special world premiere performance you've all experienced. (See *On Contemporary Plays*)

And ideally, they're still applauding while you've returned the dressing room, collected your valuables, put on your civilian clothes, and made it to the bar.

THOUGHTS ON LIVING

Morning Practice

At some point every morning I bring my hands to my heart and say
"Kind actions." Then I hold my hands to my lips and say "Kind words."
And then I hold my hands to my forehead and say "Kind thoughts."
And then I say "For myself and others."

At this point I need to wake up about three hours before I have to be
anywhere. Three hours that are mine. I'm not necessarily a morning
person but I've become one. It's my foundation for the day. I work out,
walk the dog, drink coffee, listen to a podcast.

With a morning practice, before you've done anything else, or given all
the parts of you away to everyone else, you get to hold something that's
your own.

The life of a freelancer is chaotic. You have to find the ways to create
structure and ritual. Growing up, my mother put dinner on the table
every single night. She planned the menu in advance, shopped for it, and
provided. Always salad, a starch, a protein, a vegetable. When I had kids
I thought, wow, I am going to fail at that family meal task. And then I
remembered that no one makes plays at 7am so we can always do
breakfast!

Creating your own routine is important. I've handwritten letters daily.
Meditated. Get a 5-year journal where you just write a few lines a day.
Take the time to think about what would make you feel set up for

———

success for your day. Do you need to lie still and quietly? Make a big breakfast? Call a friend?

Once you've found your routine, you'll continue to adjust it. Your needs will change. One of my favorite things about my morning routine is that I can take it with me everywhere, like my suitcase of values. (See: *My Invisible Suitcase.*) Whether I'm directing a play in Minnesota or on vacation in North Carolina, I can still practice this morning routine.

Be Astonished

I recently had the honor of spending an afternoon with the soon-to-be-BFA-Acting-graduates at Brooklyn College. In the raw vulnerable space that is 72 hours before your graduation they welcomed me on wooden benches, under a big old tree, on an unrivaled Spring day. The head of their program, the absolutely singular Patrick Sabongui, had invited me to just "chat."

Zara, an artist with a twinkle in their eye and a tender ferocity that seems beyond their years, asked me: How do you cultivate a point-of-view? And, thus, this chapter was born.

Look up.
Look out.
What do you see?
Engage your senses.

Right now, I can smell the wings I'm attempting to cook for my son. Looking out on my balcony, the waning sun is dusting the apartment building across the way with a glow that completely changes my perspective. My basil plant is wilting in the heat. Luciano's *Sweep Over My Soul* is playing from my kitchen speaker. My compression socks are making my calves feel embraced.

That is point-of-view. The way you encounter the world around you. And within that, your tastes and preferences begin to emerge. What makes you uniquely you begins to surface.

Make a list of your **likes**. Make a list of your **dislikes**. This is also point-of-view. It belongs to only you. It is personal. And it's from this place we make all of our decisions, and we create our work.

My point here is- don't miss a minute. Take notice. Listen to Mary Oliver:

> Instructions for living a life.
>
> Pay attention.
>
> Be astonished.
>
> Tell about it.

I promise you that we're interested.

Starting Out

I had a really difficult time titling this essay because I believe we're always "starting out." Every first rehearsal is the very first time. Even having done this job for 30 years I'm working with people and companies and communities for the first time. I "start out" constantly.

We're never trying to land one show, one role, one job. We're trying to build relationships. Networking often feels gross. Striking the balance between small talk and deep talk about one's art always leaves me feeling like a socially inept weirdo. So how do we do it?

I landed in Chicago in 1995 and I knew no one, had a "fake" internship (the unpaid part was not fake), and was overpaying for a Gold Coast apartment with a view of the lake. Convinced by the very convincing Curt Columbus and MaryAnn Thebus to try my luck in Chicago where there were 150 theater companies, plenty of Midwestern sky, and affordable rents, I stayed. I stayed for 20 years.

Armed with no friends and very little money, I started to attend the storefront theatre. I loved it. And when I really loved it, I wrote a handwritten letter, put a stamp on it, and mailed it to the address in the program. These letters contained my paltry resume and my considerable enthusiasm. I offered to work the box office, clean the bathroom, just freaking hang out for chrissakes. Not one person wrote me back.

My next plan was to deep dive. Identify a theatre I loved, see every play there, and eventually develop a relationship. There's a company called

Timeline Theatre in Chicago which is a great example. It was started by friends who went to the Theatre School of DePaul who wanted to continue making great work together. They had an amazing purpose and mission: TimeLine Theatre Company presents stories inspired by history that connect with today's social and political issues. I thought- BINGO I found my people. But they already had their people.

So, I saw every play. For two seasons. And eventually reached out to the Artistic Director PJ Powers and said "hey, I've seen every play for two years here and I love your theater. Can we meet?" We did. I had a pile of plays, none of which Timeline to this day has ever done. But what did happen at that lunch is that PJ I started a conversation, which is now about 20 years in the running. He invited me to attend dress rehearsals and share thoughts with him, to meet company members, to share in the traditional beer and pizza of those special nights. Eventually it felt like home. And then I was ready to direct a play there. And when I did direct there, we all already knew how to talk to each other. We shared collaborator language. One play led to the next. Until I became an Artistic Associate.

I share this because forming these relationships that repeat, that are sustained, that grow deeper- this is where we truly grow as artists. One-offs are cool, sure. Especially when they pay. But being a part of community and understanding their constituents is where we really thrive.

So, starting out, yeah, it's tough. Put in the work. Put in the time. Build the relationships. Be authentic.

Joy and Rigor

I often describe my process as equal parts JOY and RIGOR.

JOY. Take great pleasure in the work. Find times to laugh. Have dinner break dance parties. Shoot the shit. Spend the first twenty minutes of rehearsal describing the hilarity you observed online at the supermarket. Make big, silly choices in the work. Try again. Fall down. Try again. Love each other. Smile a lot. Call people by their names. Ask if you've forgotten. Smile again. Sing funny songs to your cast mates. Play practical jokes on stage management. Love your job.

RIGOR. Strive for excellence. Nothing is ever "good enough." Have the discipline to do the work. You can start with broad strokes but don't forget the details. Keep a daily practice. Start on time. Respect boundaries. Respect your co-workers. Work until you think it's finished and then keep working. Listen and take notes from your audiences, your bosses, and your peers. Try some more. Hold others accountable. Hold yourself accountable.

I've found that when I'm directing really complex pieces with heavy emotional weight and profound intellectual heft, we need a lot of joy in process. A collective way to breathe together. While working on a comedy requires a discipline and a rigor in order to get the timing correct. In both instances, both are required. We should bring these ingredients to our process as well as our product. And to our lives.

When I was directing *Disgraced* on Broadway I worked with the veteran genius stage manager, Billy Barnes. As Billy was attempting to understand my process he said "Oh, I get it. The same amount of time other people spend stressing out you spend fucking around. You still get the same amount of work done."

I smile. A lot. Which I think, at times, sends a mixed message. I'm awful at firing people or breaking up with them. Recently a colleague mentioned to me how much they admired in me a certain tone or attitude which expresses "Do not mistake my kindness for weakness." I think about this when I think about Joy and Rigor. Do not let the Joy confuse you. We're still working incredibly hard here.

Four Words Beginning with I

Inspiration. Imitation. Integration. Innovation.

The first "I" is Inspiration. We are inspired by our teachers, our mentors, other artists. We see their work and it makes us want to work. We are inspired by the world around us, by nature, by artwork, by history. We are inspired by human stories and current events.

The second "I" is Imitation. In our learning we attempt to imitate, to capture what inspired us in the first place. We strive to perfect it. Perhaps we are inspired by a drawing of an apple- we then attempt to recreate that drawing to the best of our ability. It's much like doing the scales in practicing the piano. We develop muscles this way. We are imitating the modeled behavior of our teachers, our icons, our collaborators.

In the practice of that Imitation, we move to the third "I"- Integration. This is the stage where we put our own selves, and our current moment, into the original, thus transforming it. The original apple drawing that inspired us has now been made into something else because it is part what it once was, part what I have added to it.

The fourth "I"- the holy grail- is Innovation, where something wholly new emerges. And perhaps serves as Inspiration for the next generation.

Always Beginning

Mark Rylance: *I'm always trying to clear my memory of what happened the night before. You, the audience, don't want leftovers; you don't want what I served the night before. Since we are not microwaving our genius from the day before, therefore we have the opportunity to always begin.*

It is surprising to us both that I include in this section a contemporary interpretation of a Benedictine prayer as I am not "religious" per se and if I am anything, it's a Jewish Buddhist.

At the beginning of each day, after we open our eyes to receive the light of that day,
As we listen to the voices and sounds that surround us,
We must resolve to treat each hour as the rarest of gifts,
and be grateful for the consciousness that allow us to experience it,
recalling in thanks that our awareness is a present from we know not where, or how,
or why.

When we rise from sleep let us rise for the joy of the true work that we will be about this day,
and considerately cheer one another on.
Life will always provide matters for concern.
Each day, however, brings with it reasons for joy.

Every day carries the potential to bring the experience of heaven;
Have the courage to expect good from it.

John McQuiston II, from *Always We Begin Again*

Back to beginnings. What didn't work in rehearsal one day can be tried new the next. "Sleeping on it" is always a great idea. This ties into my idea that a play is a "world premiere" every night. Whether it's *Hedda Gabler* or a-brand-new-play-by-your-best-friend-from-grad-school-that-no-one-has-ever-heard-of, it is the very first time ever, each night, that that particular audience will gather in that particular spot, with that particular barometric pressure, mixed with current events, seasoned with the events of the artists' days. We've all had the feeling of trying to recreate something that felt great the day before- whether it was in a classroom, a work setting, in a personal relationship, in a performance. And we've all seen, time and time again, that re-creation is nearly impossible. Something about it will always feel stale, used.

In *Disgraced* by Ayad Akhtar there is a dinner party that, let's just say, goes awry (no spoilers here!) Two of the dinner guests have brought a banana pudding for a dessert offering. In the play, they don't make it to the eating of the pudding. I would often say to those two actors (in multiple productions) "Tonight's the night you are going to get to eat that banana pudding!" This idea of beginning also helps spare us the dreadful note of

"Don't play the ending." Meaning, don't go into this dinner party scene knowing it's going to end in disaster, go in with the optimism and expectation that all will go as planned and of course we will eat this ridiculously delicious banana pudding (did I mention it's from Magnolia Bakery?) I've always found the "don't play the ending" note challenging. First of all, it's framed in the negative. Secondly, we *know* the ending- avoiding just feels false! Instead, we can focus our energies on beginning, rather than pretending the ending is a mystery to us. When focused on the beginning we allow anything to happen, trusting the story will unfold as it must. Or not. Otherwise, we have to try to get our scene partner back into our 10 Minute Play (see: *Whose Play Is It Anyway?*)

This is true in personal relationships as well- deciding the relationship is going to end in tears, disaster, heartbreak doesn't give you much opportunity to actually experience it in the present moment. When we are so busy writing ahead in the narrative we limit possible outcomes. We see this manifest itself not only in rehearsal, but in our homes, our other workspaces, our elections.

And that's the key, right? We desperately desire to be in the present. This is the holy grail of performance. These are also the most blissful moments in life, when we are present in our work, with our loved ones, with ourselves. It is becoming more and more apparent to me that these vital lessons which I am learning in the rehearsal room, in the crucible of tech, in the painful relinquishing of power on opening night, are endlessly applicable to the actual task of living.

We must learn to forgive ourselves our misdeeds, our dropped lines, our errors in judgment both on and off the stage. We get to begin again each day, each performance. And in beginning again, we remain present and ready for discovery. *Have the courage to expect good from it.*

The Eighth Day

Who made the rules about this seven-day week?!

When I'm in charge of everything, I'm changing the calendar. Enough of this seven-day week, we need eight. But on the eighth day, no one works. We might have to have alternating eighth days so life functions but I haven't figured that part out yet. The important part is that we all have one.

On the eighth day, you can't work. You can't do laundry. You can't run errands. It is a day for getting through the list. The list of things that have been recommended to you by people you love and respect! Podcast listening, movie watching, book reading. All those articles you've saved.

It is necessary to our work and to our human development to take in all of these things. These are the cornerstones to our conversations and to our evolution. We cannot create (or live) in a vacuum. And in this fast-paced life we have no time for these. They feel extra yet they are imperative.

Start an "8th day list."

Changing Your Grip

I play tennis. I recommend that everyone find a way to use their body, this tremendous gift of which we are stewards from birth to death. Also, get out of your head and into your body. Plus, I've made great friends with people who don't even know what the theatre is, some of whom might even read and enjoy this book. You can learn a lot about yourself by playing tennis. For instance, today my coach, Chris, said to me "You are trying to do too many difficult things at once." Chris is very wise.

Yesterday I decided to change my forehand grip. The forehand is the most used stroke in tennis and most people have a stronger forehand than a backhand. Not me. I realized I've been holding the racquet incorrectly for most of my life. I heard a voice from my past calling to me "Shake hands with the racquet." So, I did, and it became clear that my grip was…wrong. It's really difficult to change something when you're 51 years old but since my tennis game is a pretty low risk situation, I thought I'd give it a whirl.

It feels really awkward to hold the racquet differently. And in a domino effect it actually changed my backhand (now I switch grips differently), my volleys (I'm not switching my grip) and my serves (I can recover faster into my forehand after serving.) I also can see how tightly I'm holding on, like my racquet is my boyfriend from college with one foot out the door. It's also changing my perspective on the game itself.

I am engaging in a new way, focusing on how hold the racquet. I don't know that this is an improvement but it's definitely a new way of seeing. I wish I could tell you I'm ready for Roland Garros, but I have not seen that much difference in my game, just my perspective.

What would happen if we changed our "grip"? Saw and used our tools in a new way? Would we notice something else, something new, something different? What would happen if we *loosened* our grip? My racquet has not flown out of my hand yet. And the boyfriend from my college years, I was definitely better off when he had both feet out the door.

See you on the court.

My Invisible Suitcase

When my kids were younger, I told them they carried an invisible suitcase full of their values wherever they went. I define values as what principles are most important to us that then act as an engine for our choices. Human beings, on the whole, share the same values. What makes us different is which values are leading, what is packed on the top of that suitcase. Throughout the course of our lives which values lead is bound to change. In my 20's, values like *recognition*, *adventure*, and *independence* took the lead. So, I moved to Chicago, spent six months traveling in India, and started a theater company. Now in my 50's I am driven by *financial security*, *creating legacy*, and *fulfillment*. So, I make job decisions differently, am teaching and mentoring more, and prioritizing friends and family time.

It's a wonderful exercise to think about what values are leading you at any given moment. Most fascinating, and complex, is that oftentimes you have to compromise one value for another to be satisfied. For instance, if I am being led by my *ambition*, I might have to compromise *family* a little.

I started talking about values in the rehearsal room during my production of Sam Shepard's *Buried Child* at Writers Theatre in 2018. Those characters make some bizarre choices, but why? Understanding the values driving Halie to keep so many secrets affects the intentions of the character and gives some clues to the actor playing the role. Her *integrity* might be compromised but her *control* is satisfied.

Actors can struggle with characters that are less than savory. No one wants to play Hitler, a slave owner, or Dick Cheney. Our stories need these characters though. It is how we chronicle and learn from our history. (More on this topic in *Why We Do It.*) The values exercise is a great way to understand why people do bad things. Hitler was trying to save Germany and *effectiveness* seems to have been a core value. Having actors think about three values that might guide their character can become a great shorthand for making choices in scenework as well as creating greater understanding of intentions. It also helps with the Venn diagram of character and actor by identifying which values they may have in common and where they differ.

Here's a partial list of values that are great engines for intentions:

Truth	Peace	Empathy
Curiosity	Loyalty	Freedom
Power	Love	Risk
Courage	Family	Purpose
Happiness	Prosperity	Justice
Honor	Order	Growth
Community	Spirituality	Prestige

Sundowning

And sometimes it's time to call it. No matter how much time is "left."

At some point in my 40s I realized I had been accidentally treating directing like an hourly job, especially in rehearsal. I felt like I had to use all of my rehearsal hours in order to be paid. Or else get sent to the Principal's Office. I began to see not all plays and not all rooms need the same thing. The way the American Theatre is still set up (haven't solved this one yet) there is a bit of a cut and paste that occurs when calendaring shows. I'm sure this has to do with many important factors other than what the rehearsal room needs. Oftentimes we don't even know what we need ahead of time so it would be impossible to do this calculus. So, we end up with a pretty standard schedule. Inevitably this means sometimes we will want *more* time (most of the time) and sometimes we just don't need all that time.

When I started the process for Yasmina Reza's << *ART* >> at the Guthrie I had four whole weeks of rehearsal until tech, six days a week, eight hours a day. For those of you unfamiliar, << *ART* >> is a three-hander and my design was a unit set. I thought "what the hell am I going to do with all of those hours?" It turns out we used them ALL. I staged the show in a few days but then we used the time to elevate the play from three dudes talking about art to something that felt more transcendent and more of an experience. We had the time to take the play apart and put it back together again. We asked challenging questions of ourselves about the relationships in the play and our relationship to them. This is a great example of you never know the time you need.

On the other hand, when rehearsing Paloma Nozicka's *Enough to Let the Light In* at Contemporary American Theatre Festival, a suspenseful, queer love story, we often ended the day a few hours early. The two actors have a pre-existing friendship, I've worked with them both multiple times. The play is delicate in a way that it didn't want too much decided, or too much rehearsal time, so we used that extra time for bike rides and visits to the Mennonite meat market. When in West Virginia…

According to the Mayo Clinic "The term "sundowning" refers to a state of confusion that occurs in the late afternoon and lasts into the night. Sundowning can cause various behaviors, such as confusion, anxiety, aggression or ignoring directions. Sundowning also can lead to pacing or wandering. Sundowning isn't a disease." It's typically found in homes for Elderly Care and in babies. And also rehearsal rooms.

These are the moments when we have hit the wall. An actor is frustrated or we all can't stop giggling or no one can maintain focus. The stage manager forgets to reset the scene. I get frustrated with myself and everyone and can feel the heat rising in my body. My inner critic gets really loud in those moments. I suddenly feel like a hack, completely unprofessional. Why can't I finish out the workday? There is no point in working anymore. We have officially sundowned and may cause more harm than good.

In the very same production of << *ART* >> we had one day where I did call it early. Patrick Sabongui, truly one of the most nimble actors with whom I have ever worked, was really struggling with the character of Marc.

There was a chasm for him between himself and the character, plus it was an instance where I stepped in late in the game to direct the play and hadn't cast it myself. So, there was an added level of insecurity on Patrick's part because I hadn't "chosen" him. I kept giving Patrick similar versions of the same note (sorry, Patrick!) and he knew he wasn't getting what I was after. I wanted him to let loose more, to explore anger, to react from his gut. We sundowned- there was definitely confusion and anxiety- so I called it a day. I then asked Patrick to go for a walk with me and Kode (my incredible dog who travels all over with me.) On our two hour walk we got to the core of the issue. As an Egyptian man, Patrick didn't want to express his anger on stage for fear of fulfilling a stereotype. In a setting that wasn't the rehearsal room we were able to parse the issue, having a meaningful discussion, build trust, and felt ready to get back in the room and attack the work with a new fervor and integrity.

No matter how hard corporate America and the patriarchy have tried, it's impossible to put a linear shape on the making of art. I think the generous six day a week, eight hour a day schedule actually creates a huge protective bubble on time. I'd love to start viewing that time as a cushion should I need it, rather than a mandate from "The Man."

A piece of advice I got when my babies were young- if they're screaming bloody murder, change their environment. I remember rocking baby Noah in zero-degree Chicago winter attempting to follow this advice. It also works in the rehearsal room.

Getting Personal

Making our work is personal. We must be deeply invested. It's one of the hallmarks of artistry, how much we invest. How do we do that and protect ourselves?

When collaborating, develop a vocabulary that extends beyond the rehearsal room. Go see other plays, go to a museum, go for long walks. Talk about other art together. When Ayad Akhtar and I were making seven productions of his Pulitzer Prize winning play *Disgraced* as well as developing *The Who and The What* we spent many hours together, in rehearsal and out. We took walks, ate meals, went to the movies. We told stories about our fathers. We shared our love of Philip Roth. We talked about the complex notions of identity and about being American. These conversations ultimately modeled an honesty and transparency that we brought into the rehearsal room and affected all of our collaborators. Being vulnerable was possible for everyone because the two leaders modeled that behavior.

One day, we were in San Diego, we went to see the Spike Jonze's deeply prescient film, *Her*. Ayad and I did not see eye to eye about this movie. At all. I was hung up on the male gaze, objectification of women, that she didn't even need a BODY for god's sake for him to obsess over her. Ayad was struck by the potential of AI, the camera angles, the artistry of Jonze's work. In a scintillating discussion we were able to open each other's eyes to other ideas. Neither of us had made the work so we felt free to criticize and talk freely without it getting personal. Which gave us vocabulary to then use in the rehearsal room. We were learning how to debate, how to express our opinions, in a neutral space. This conversation, and others like it, where we discussed other people's work affected the way we were able to talk about our own work. We had a sense of each other's aesthetic and preferences. We had a shared vocabulary.

The best way for this personal work to occur comes from an engine of curiosity. Pay attention. Notice things in one another. Ask questions. It's one of the reasons I love collaborating with people who are different than me. I can make no assumptions! Everything becomes an investigation. When Ellen Fairey and I were working on her play *Support Group For Men*, we were asked no less than two million times why these two women were making this play about this group of Chicago guys. I would reply "I've been studying them my whole life."

Simone Weil wrote "Attention is the rarest and purest form of generosity." This is what this personal work requires. You know how special it is to feel "chosen"? Someone *picked* me. What it feels like to be in someone's particular gaze. That's so much the job of the director. It's also the job of the actor for the scene partner. What happens when we really *see* each other.

Create holistic relationships, create trust.

How to Be Big and Small

I want to transform what power looks like.

When I first started directing, I had no idea how to be in "power" in the room. Most of the directors I knew were men, so I felt like in order to have power I had to act like a man. So, I threw on a baseball hat and stood with my legs spread a little further than I normally would and thought "is this it? Is this power?" It didn't sit right on me or make sense in my body. Plus, I was performing being a director, rather than actually doing it. (See: *Finding the Bones* - I had yet to realize that I didn't have to play status, I had it.)

I hadn't found my female role models yet and when I did, I was quite shocked that none of them wore baseball hats on the regular. Lisa Banes looked damn good in one but that was saved for Dodgers games. Lisa led with an enormous amount of class and grace. Mary Ann Thebus led with her humor and her casual nature. And I watched the way Martha Lavey could hold power in a room. It was often with her silence and her observation. Her waiting to speak, rather than taking up space. None of these elements were particularly gendered but none of them looked like power I had ever seen before. All three of these women led from what felt true to them and that was how I learned what true power looks like.

I learned a painful lesson from Martha. I was producing the First Look Series of New Plays at Steppenwolf Theatre (a now defunct program which produced three workshop productions of new plays while providing access to audience members of the process.) The offices for

Steppenwolf were across the street from the theatre and Martha and I were frequently making that Frogger-like journey together. One day she stopped in the middle of the double yellow lines adorning the center of Halsted.

Martha: Kimberly. I don't understand what you're saying.

Me: What do you mean?

Martha: You punctuate all of your sentences with a question mark.

Me: I do?

Martha: Yes. You do that in order to appear harmless. Don't. I know you aren't going to harm me. And you lose meaning when you punctuate inappropriately.

So, the next day, we're crossing Halsted again. And Martha stops.

Martha: Kimberly. Stop yelling at me.

Me: What!

Martha: You've been yelling at me all day.

Me: No! I haven't!

Martha: You have.

Me: I am just trying to punctuate appropriately!!

Lesson learned. I'm most fascinated by my desire to appear "harmless." The "excuse me, pardon me" of it all. This punctuation lesson taught me to stand in my opinions, sit comfortably in my intelligence.

And then I had the enormous privilege of directing the singular Harvey Fierstein in his play *Bella Bella* about the legendary politician and human,

Bella Abzug. Not only did I get to spend time with my heroes Gloria Steinem, Lily Tomlin and Marlo Thomas, but I also got to do a very deep dive into the life and leadership of Bella. One of my favorite quotes from her:

"Women will change the nature of power, rather than power changing the nature of women."

That blew me away! I realized I had been perceiving *power* as a dirty word. People with power were men, were wealthy, didn't care about art or women or babies. They were the 1% and the enemy. Bella redefined the word for me and my opportunity to transform myself as a leader. I noticed that a lot of my behaviors that I was already doing were, in fact, what power looked like on me.

I was directing Laura Eason's *Sex With Strangers* at The Geffen Playhouse in Los Angeles which was, at that time, under the leadership of Steppenwolf ensemble member, Randall Arney. Randy had known me since I was 21 years old and first arrived at Steppenwolf. He definitely was having a difficult time wrapping his head around the fact that I was old enough to direct a play. One day he popped into my rehearsal while I was giving notes. I was sitting on the floor and my actors and stage management team were all sitting in chairs. I finished going through the checkboxes in my notebook and went over to say hi to Randy.

Randy: Wow, how do you do that?

Me: What?

Randy: Give notes while sitting on the floor!

Me: That's where I'm most comfortable.

Randy: And they were all listening to you!

Me: Well, yeah, I'm the director. I'm giving them information they need.
It doesn't matter where I am sitting.

It hadn't occurred to Randy that you don't have to stand legs akimbo,
under a baseball hat, during notes. I was transforming what power
looked like.

This is ongoing work for me. Especially in a world with such an
imbalance of power where we are constantly attempting to reorganize
our structures- from the social to the institutional- to better reflect the
world we actually inhabit; it is essential that *power* isn't something to solve
or achieve but rather to examine and understand it's mighty privilege and
responsibility.

A text I refer to a lot, and attempt to achieve, is from my constant
"companion", Pema Chödron.

BEING BIG AND SMALL AT THE SAME TIME

I was once invited to teach with the Sakyong Mipham Rinpoche, my
teacher's eldest son, in a situation where it wasn't exactly clear what my
status was. Sometimes I was treated as a big deal who should come in
through a special door and sit in a special seat. Then I'd think, "Okay,
I'm a big deal." I'd start running with that idea and come up with big-deal
notions about how things should be.

Then I'd get the message, "Oh, no, no, no. You should just sit on the floor and mix with everybody and be one of the crowd." Okay. So now the message was that I should just be ordinary, not set myself up or be the teacher. But as soon as I was getting comfortable with being humble, I would be asked to do something special that only big deals did.

This was a painful experience because I was always being insulted and humiliated by my own expectations. As soon as I was sure how it should be, so I could feel secure, I would get a message that it should be the other way. Finally, I said to the Sakyong, "This is really hurting. I just don't know who I'm supposed to be," and he said, "Well, you have to learn to be big and small at the same time."

I am learning that it's just as powerful to have the answers as it is to say "I don't know." That power can be kind, vulnerable, and generous. It's an ongoing process.

Finding the Extraordinary in the Ordinary

Attention is the sincerest form of generosity. To shine a light on someone or something is such a gift. In our work, whatever that work may be, we have the opportunity to imbue big meaning into something seemingly small. On my windowsill I have a collection of ephemera- a piece of driftwood from a walk on the Washington State coast, a matchbook from the bar across from my housing when working in Boston, a rock my daughter gave me. Each one of these tells a story rich with humanity, memory and love. They mark specific moments in my life and my growth. By keeping these objects, holding them in my hand, I make them sacred.

"By taking care of ordinary things- our pots and pans, our clothing, our teeth- we rejoice in them." Pema Chödrön

This is what we can do not only in our lives but also in the theatre. We can marvel in small wonders and highlight these miracles. Giving specificity to relationship and human behavior honors it. Nothing tickles me more than an actor discovering a detail- chewing on a toothpick or the way a husband studies a freckle on his beloved's shoulder. Making our theatrical environments specific, paying attention to those details enriches our work.

What I want to insist upon is *curiosity*. None of this exists without our genuine curiosity in humans and how humans behave.

They See Me Standing

Mentorship is truly my life's work.

It may seem daunting to find a mentor. Start by considering who you admire. Send them a note. See if they'd be willing to meet you for coffee. Look to build a relationship, not just assist in a limited time frame. True mentorship is an exchange. I think about my relationship with Marti Lyons (who wrote the introduction!) I can hardly call myself Marti's mentor anymore but back in 2009 I was. She had reached out and it took us months to finally connect. And once we did, we never stopped! Marti assisted me on several shows in one season- a season in which I had recently gotten divorced and was raising a two-year-old and a six-month-old by myself. In between rehearsals Marti and I talked about plays, we ran errands, we talked about our love lives. We discussed leadership and being women and our big dreams. We shared our fears and secrets and made a lot of really great work.

One of the shows Marti assisted me on was *The Letters* at Writers Theatre. I had tried to get in the door there for years. The Artistic Director had difficulty remembering my name, let alone that I was a director. I cornered him in a theater lobby and insisted he get to know me. It took a long time but eventually he did get to know me. I didn't want the path to take that long for Marti and I asked him to meet with her. A few seasons later I had one of my proudest moments when I received the season brochure from Writers. Marti and I were both directing there in the same season.

I am passionate about my work as a director. I am even more passionate about the longevity of our field, our ability to tell stories that reflect the ever-changing world around us. Although mentorship can be seen as an act of kindness or generosity, I view it as a necessity, a responsibility. If we are to continue to make work, to tell stories, or even survive another 50, 100, 1000 years, we need to raise up this next generation.

So how do we do this? We hold open doors. Doors can be heavy and unwieldy. Some doors are closed due to impossible entry fees, some are closed by gender barriers, racial prejudices. Some are so tightly shut by an older generation so afraid of what these brilliant young people have to say. We must kick these doors down, pry them open.

What else can we do? We can bear witness. Mentorship, for me, is about seeing. It is not an Act of Doing, but an Act of Seeing. Seeing you. I see you there. In the shadows, in the wings, in the back of the classroom. It is my job as a mentor to shine a light and hold the mirror up. To see the potential and the possibility. To hold some of their burden, to free up their hands for the doing.

What else? On days where it feels like too much work, where I work twice as hard for half as much, where I feel like making art, raising kids, earning a living, being a friend daughter sister parent athlete artist teacher director is just too much…
Days where I want to lie down, pull the covers over my head and wait for the storm to pass…I stand back up. I stand up because they are all watching. I stand up for Ashley and Sharifa. Kate and Addie.

Brooke and Pascale and Emma and Marti and Keira and Nate and Skye. I stand up for Noah and Delaney. They make me stronger and better and braver. And they see me standing. And they are stronger and better and braver for it.

Advancing and Expanding

We hear a lot that great artists are also great thieves. I like to think we take an idea that's been established and advance and expand it. In Joshua Wolf Shenk's incredible book *Powers of Two* where he discusses the multitude of ways in which partnerships thrive, he highlights the "Resonator/Generator" relationship. In this relationship one person has an idea, it hurtles forward into space and the collaborator responds to it, thusly making something new that exists between them. I imagine a gyroscope, forever spinning, emitting energy at every turn.

These gyroscope moments exist all around us. They're on the playground when one child establishes the "pirate ship" and another spots a distant "island." They're in the classroom when one student excavates a symbol in the text and another then unlocks deeper meaning. They're in the rehearsal room between an actor and director.

I am most excited about the notion of advancing and expanding when I think about how we advance and expand culture, the way we work, how our work is viewed in the world, how we envision change. Bella Abzug said "we aren't looking to *transfer* power but to *transform* it." What does that transformation look like?

I love listening to Julia Louis Dreyfus' podcast *Wiser Than Me*. In each hour-long episode, Dreyfuss has a conversation with a woman she deems wiser than herself. This a great source of inspiration for advancing and expanding. Listening to women like Carol Burnett and Gloria Steinem talking about how they paved their paths so that we can stand on their great shoulders and go even further.

I was having lunch with a young, female director who asked me how I made my way in the male dominated theater field. I told her I smiled and nodded a lot. She looked at me, as if she was dropped to earth to save me and said, "You'll never have to smile and nod again." And I said to her "No, you'll never have to smile and nod because I did it for you."

What does this have to do with institutional change? Working inside institutions and trying to get, well, anything done often feels like attempting to change the course of the Titanic. These predominantly white spaces have been doing the same thing for a long time. As has the Patriarchy. As has this Democracy. I love bringing the notion of advancing and expanding to these bigger ideas. How can we take what exists, mine the good from it, and build from there?

I've been a freelance director for… a long time (28 years at the writing of this edition.) I've described what I do as "itinerant leadership." We aren't only creating culture in our rehearsal rooms but we are also responsible for what we bring to the institution. Like the national park system, I like to leave theatres better than I found them. That means to me creating a holistic energy and message surrounding the production while empowering everyone (from house management to scenic designer to artistic director) to do their jobs really well because they are armed with the knowledge of my vision and access to my process. This is as much about the content of the play as it is about what the audience leaves the theatre talking about as it is the vibes in my rehearsal room.

Do not underestimate your ability to advance and expand notions in all of the rooms you are in.

1. **Always make your own art.** Don't sit around waiting for someone to ask you to make art for them. Be creating. It doesn't have to be on a big stage, it can be in your living room. Having friends over to read Christopher Marlowe's *Tamburlaine* in your living room because you never read it is making art. Or try other art. I took pottery classes when pregnant with my oldest, Noah, and didn't stop 'til my belly made it so I couldn't reach the wheel. If you do this, you won't atrophy. I was speaking recently with a graduate of the MFA Directing Program at Brooklyn College. Since graduating she set herself a "learning goal" for each month. One month she endeavored to learn more about making musical theatre. Another month she dove into studying how we create controlled chaos on stage. In this way, she was always growing and becoming more of an artist. If you do any of these things you won't feel sorry for yourself when you feel like opportunity isn't coming your way.

2. **Always be in the service of someone else's art.** Have a phone conversation with a friend about what they're working on. Help out at the box office of a colleague's brand-new theater. Attend someone else's rehearsal and give notes. Assist. If you do this, you will always be learning. If you do this, you can notice process in a way in which you can't be present when making your own work. If you do this, you're also feeding energy into the notion of creation and prioritizing art in our culture.

3. **Always do something that has nothing to do with your art.** I'm a fitness junkie (which I highly recommend for your mental

and physical health.) Distance running, yoga, tennis, treadmill classes, lifting weights. I also love to travel, to cook, to read. Go to a concert. Work on home improvement. Pema Chödron talks about attention to the details. During the pandemic I spent so much time taking care of small details, caring for my plants, making elaborate recipes for my children. These tasks might be adjacent to art making but they use the brain in a different way. Plus, you're nourishing a more interesting person and a better artist by getting out of the vacuum (and into vacuuming.) Included in this rule is having friends who are "civilians." There's more to talk about than auditions, why our unions aren't better, and what shows we've seen recently.

This #3 is the most important of all the rules. It is a means of survival in a complex and competitive world. I understand the importance of self-care, an occasional massage, sleeping in. Following these three rules as a practice will create a sustained sense of humanity and clarity in you so that you are able to bring your best self to the work.

You're Not Who You Used to Be

My dear friend and brilliant actor Behzad Dabu and I were having a conversation one day and were speaking about the dreams of our younger selves. Behzad had always wanted to be in a play at Steppenwolf. When Behzad was younger he didn't think about the myriad of theaters this country holds. Nor was dreaming of being a series regular on a television show something he thought was for him as a Zoroastrian Indian kid growing up in Syracuse.

As the universe will unfold in her own particular way, Behzad ended up being a regular on a major television show playing Simon Drake for three seasons on *How to Get Away with Murder*. Not a dream he had conceived but pretty dreamy in the long run. And Behzad has worked, and continues to, all over the country. Just not at Steppenwolf. Yet. We need to readjust our dreams as our horizons broadened.

Another point that Behzad and I discussed is that the Steppenwolf he dreamed of as a child has changed and evolved as much as Behzad had. It's not the same institution, nor is Behzad the same actor, so we need to renew our commitments to our dreams. Do we still want to make those same vows years later?

As we age our view of the world expands as do the possibilities contained therein. Remember when you thought being ten whole years old, double digits!, was going to exponentially expand your universe? Try being fifty.

Our dreams require the same malleability, adaptability and flexibility that our life requires. Growing up, the models I had were all two parents and some number of kids living in the suburbs. Moms mostly stayed home. I'm a single, working mom raising two kids by myself. I had to adjust my ideas of what the dreams were when my world expanded to include different models.

My daughter and I recently traveled to Italy. We had a glorious eight days, ate our weight in pasta, she discovered mojitos (I know, in Italy, who'd of thunk it?) and missed our connecting flight at Heathrow. For whatever reason we couldn't get home for about 48 hours. We had to shift the dream of our beds at home and re-envision what the next few days would hold. At first, I was so frustrated by not being able to accomplish all the tasks I was hoping to do upon my return. It was making me grumpy. I realize being stranded in London for two days doesn't exactly suck, but it was different than my plans. When I let go of this rigidity, I was able to embrace the trip. We had a great day at the Tate Modern, I got to see a play I loved at the Old Vic, we visited some friends and I got to show Delaney where I lived when I studied abroad thirty years ago. Not bad for a shifted dream.

Life isn't only what you see- we need to push the boundaries of what's possible to dream for ourselves. Dreams are meant to be expansive.

Having It All

I've been a freelance director now for more than half of my life. That means for more than half of my life I've been my own boss. I control my calendar, I live by my ethics, I decide which jobs I take and which I don't. I even choose my collaborators most of the time. I travel all over the country, living my best life in corporate housing, using ClassPass to try out every fitness cult on the planet, and have had lovers in multiple cities. My children are truly being raised by a Village and travel to see their mom at work, a resilient and dynamic leader who tells stories that change lives and create conversation in multiple markets.

I even get to continue growing as an artist, trying out new mediums, such as scripted audio podcasts and directing comedy specials. I've directed everywhere from a church basement to Broadway and worked with some major talent, famous and not yet famous. All while being represented by one of the best agents in the business (Chris Till at Paradigm, who is as eager to dream with me as he is to reality check me.) I'm supported by an incredible union, 2200 strong, where I am in solidarity and celebration with the brightest minds in our field. Life is abundant.

I must look like I have it all.

Here's another version of the story. I've been a freelance director for more than half of my life. That means for more than half of my life I haven't known where my income is coming from, if I'll get paid on time, and what I will earn year to year. I have to take most jobs offered to me because of this scarcity mindset. And sometimes when I'm working on five projects all at once I'm also chasing down checks and can't pay my bills even though I've earned thousands of dollars that I can't seem to get anyone to pay me. My union protects me, but institutions are so slow to get my contracts signed and it's in my best interest to adhere to calendar deadlines because the show running behind is a detriment mainly to me. So, I start working without a contract, which also means without a paycheck.

I work inside institutions that occasionally have toxic cultures that I inherit and have to navigate for myself and the artists for whom I feel responsible. Sometimes leadership in those institutions have different ideas than I do, and I have to figure out how to honor their notes and my vision. I feel like I have thirty different bosses all at once, all of whom think I am available 24/7 to speak with them and think they're my most important project.

Sometimes the housing has cockroaches, or no internet, or the funk of thousands of artists before me. And the "gym" is a treadmill that occasionally works and mismatched free weights. The nearest grocery is a thirty-minute walk, or I can sign out the shared '84 Chevy Impala.

Meanwhile, my children *need* me. They need new shoes, a haircut. They need homework help. They need structure. The Village is cool, and all, but the Village has also ruined my favorite cast iron, gotten into fender benders in my car, broken vintage cocktail glasses, and overspent on groceries. And the village isn't Mommy. The Village can't navigate heartbreak and comfort in quite the same way or enforce that suitcase of values quite like I can.

Plus, I've got my own mother, the model Stay-At-Home-Mom, who is worried and checking in with me and checking in on the kids and I feel like I've failed her, and failed my kids, and am failing myself. And my actors don't really like each other, and I don't really like the play, and the Artistic Director is up my ass, and all I have is pickles and mustard in my company housing.

Always a great moment to remember I'm professionally single, that I don't have a real partner, that help is NOT on the way. That I hold the weight of it all.

But I have it all, right?

"Be kind for everyone is fighting a great battle." Yep. True. Every maxim rings true. "The grass is always greener." Like in any profession, any life, there are good days and bad days. I think about one of my favorite children's books *Alexander and the Terrible, Horrible, No Good, Very Bad Day.* We all have those days.

I'm learning to not hide these days. I always feel guilty complaining, asking for help, asking for comfort. Because I have so much. Lately, I've realized that sharing these feelings also helps others. It's rare that we're all having a bad day at the same time. There's probably room to reach out to your partner, best friend, mentee, mentor, neighbor. It feels good to help someone hold their burdens. It also feels good to know that we're not alone in these kinds of days. Weeks. Months.

Also, go to therapy. Everyone should. Not to solve a "problem." It's time that's just for you to talk about you because you are literally paying someone to listen. And if they know you on a good day, they'll be better help on a bad one.

91

So, yeah, I guess I do have it all. I have an incredible, ever-changing career that I bust my ass to do. I have two wonderful, curious, hilarious kids. I have friends and collaborators who I've grown with for decades. And I've got me. This body, this mind, this heart, this life. I've got it all.

Island Magic

Society would have us believe that endings are sad. We have so little language for grieving. Therefore, when we experience endings in our lives- the end of a rehearsal process, a run of a show, a special project, a job, a romance, a life- we feel adrift and bereft.

I find the progression that begins with leaving the rehearsal room and into the theatre very disorienting. When I'm in the rehearsal room my music stand or table is practically on top of the set. I am really in it with the actors. When we do notes, we sit together. Then when we move to the theatre, my table is in the house and a distance is created. Plus, I'm in the dark now and the actors under theatrical light. Sometimes they can't even see me. Once an audience becomes a part of our process, I need to sit even further back (mainly so they don't hear me muttering to my assistant and designers.) After opening night, I'm not even in the picture.

I spoke with my dear friend and colleague, Damon Kiely, about this very experience for his terrific book *How to Rehearse a Play.*

"If you think about perspective in drawing the play becomes bigger and you become smaller. You move to the edge of the frame, the director. A little sad. There's no place for me there anymore. It's about understanding that. We raise our children to leave us, and then we will have done a wonderful job."

I believe people come into our lives for a reason. Sometimes we can find that reason in a few short weeks (or maybe even a one-night stand!)

Sometimes it takes a lifetime for that understanding. The length of a relationship is not a measure of its value.

How do we leave these relationships with grace? How can we, in the moment of experience, understand the impact of the experience?

I officiated an amazing, special, perfect wedding on Vashon Island in 2015. A small group of people came together, lived in a former boy scout camp, took boat rides, foraged in scavenger hunts, played instruments and talked about love by the fire. It felt like living inside of an oil painting. My dear friend Nathan Hosner and I are still quite sure the Germans must have a word for that. We called it "Island Magic." We knew it was short lived and knew we needed to keep it with us for all times. We attempted to harness those moments, to store them for later use. This is one way to accept endings.

Another way is a consciousness required. I write everything down. I journal in my "big green book" for the big thoughts and I have a five year journal where I jot thoughts day to day. This is a way to think of your life and experiences on a timeline. How big is the dot? And also knowing it is a part of your larger, beautiful life.

Why We Do It

It's good for us to imagine the most we can possibly imagine
so we can begin to the move the boundaries of where we can go.
-Gloria Steinem

We, humans, are in crisis. Democracy has lost its currency. We're still not healed from a global pandemic. The next generation was raised on tiny screens. We're increasingly isolated. An article from 2022 in *Scientific American* said we're even having less sex. That can't be good. We're bereft, a civilization in grief over the loss of our moral compass.

And let's not get started on War. There is violence and senseless casualties and divides and genocides and the deep seeded effects of Colonialism happening all over the globe. The globe that's currently turning into hot lava because of hairspray and plastic and our general bad behavior.

These are big picture. On our small scale, we are in debt, getting divorced, being downsized, being reduced in every which way possible. We are getting cancer, attending funerals, seeing our trauma played out on every big and small screen that we are inundated with.

What does our work matter when our world is so dismal? After 9/11 I thought "What the fuck am I doing playing pretend for a living? Shouldn't I take these considerable skills and save the world?"

Being a human=being in crisis.

So, here's the great news. That means that's been happening since the beginning of time. That is what connects us over distance and eons. And the very best way to feel connected? Through story.

"This is a hopeful notion, because it implies that our minds are built on common architecture – that whatever is present in me might also be present in you. "I" might be a 19th-century Russian count, "you" a part-time Walmart clerk in 2017, in Boise, Idaho, but when you start crying at the end of my (Tolstoy's) story "Master and Man", you have proved that we have something in common, communicable across language and miles and time, and despite the fact that one of us is dead.

Another reason you're crying: you've just realised that Tolstoy thought well of you – he believed that his own notions about life here on earth would be discernible to you, and would move you.

Tolstoy imagined you generously, you rose to the occasion." - George Saunders

Storytelling has existed since the beginning of time, in every culture. It has been a way to spread the news, to imagine, and also to reflect. Storytelling teaches us how to live. Explores the Jurassic mess of our humanity. We gather in community to witness joy and grief and crisis and feel less alone. We gather to see all the possibilities of us play out on stage. The incredible contract with the audience- we know you're *acting* and that this is all *fake* but for these few hours I'm gonna' believe it because that investment makes me respond on an emotional level.

It's rumored that the Greeks made all those plays to teach us how to live. They zeroed in on our basest impulses, created story around them, and taught us valuable life lessons, like Don't Fuck Your Mom or You Will

Have to Blind Yourself. We've lost that a bit in our culture. Now our storytelling just mirrors us, rather than challenging us to think bigger, be bigger, do bigger.

So, I think this is why I do it, why I'm not running for office or prosecuting slumlords.

One morning last week, when we should've been designing a show, my friend and collaborator, the scenic designer Frank Oliva, and I were commiserating about our love lives. He said, "Being human isn't for the faint of heart."

In creating these stories, in seeing our impulses play out on stages in front of living, breathing humans we are attempting to heal the wound at the center of our heart break. We can't do it alone.

There's a howl at the center of every story. (I call it the howl, some call it a question, some a trauma.) I directed a production of *The Diary of Anne Frank* in the now defunct, much beloved original Writers' Theatre space, in the back of a bookstore. The scenic designer, Jack Magaw, and I wanted to be as close to the actual footprint of the attic. It was claustrophobic in there, all actors stayed on stage the whole play. There was only seating for about 50 people in the attic. One preview the show was sold out so I watched from a crappy 9" black and white monitor in the "green room"- a curtained off area in another part of the bookstore. I couldn't see very well since the play was performed in the round and the monitor only picked up one side of the theatre. The picture was grainy and I eventually lost interest and had a couple of glasses of wine. Unprofessional, sure, but then I never would've discovered this notion. The actors, after the Nazis arrive, end up back in the green room, everyone panting. I was like "wow, you all are working really hard." And I thought "Oh shit, they have to do this eight shows a week for the next six months." I realized why. And then I said "Well, if one day we all come to a solid understanding of *why* the Holocaust occurred and no longer see echoes of it in our daily lives, then we can stop making this play. But until then we need to tell and re-tell this story in an attempt to understand."

Can telling stories about ordinary people in extraordinary circumstances save the world? Maybe. When we approach our work, and our lives, with a sense of purpose, vitality, and integrity, we are modeling the society in which we want to live. Why not begin today? Smile at strangers, take care when giving feedback, explore generosity in receiving it. Notice something new, take a yoga class, write it all down. And whatever you do, do it with equal parts joy and rigor. This, all of this, is what a person would do.

Bibliography/Eighth Day List

Akhtar, Ayad. *Disgraced.* New York, New York. Back Bay Books. September 10, 2013.

Ball, David. *Backwards & Forwards: A Technical Manual for Reading Plays.* Carbondale, Illinois. Southern Illinois University Press. July 7, 1983.

Bogart, Anne. *A Director Prepares.* Abingdon, Oxfordshire. Routledge. May 24, 2001.

Brook, Peter. *The Empty Space.* New York, New York. Touchstone. January 1, 1996.

Chekhov, Anton. *Three Sisters.* Translated by Curt Columbus. Chicago, Illinois. Ivan R. Dee. April 28, 2004.

Chris Gethard: Career Suicide. Directed by Kimberly Senior, performances by Chris Gethard. HBO. 2017.

Chödrön, Pema. *The Pocket Pema Chodron (Shambhala Pocket Classics).* Boulder, Colorado. Shambhala Publications. December 9, 2008.

Dogville. Directed by Lars von Trier, performances by Nicole Kidman, Harriet Andersson, Lauren Bacall, and Jean-Marc Barr, 20th Century Studios, Lionsgate, Columbia Pictures. 2003.

Eason, Laura. *Sex With Strangers.* Dramatist. New York, New York. Dramatists Play Service, Inc. January 1, 2014.

Goodrich, Frances, and Albert Hackett. *The Diary of Anne Frank.* New York, New York. Dramatists Play Service, Inc. January 1, 1958.

Inge, William. *Come Back, Little Sheba.* New York, New York. Samuel French. January 1, 1978.

Kiely, Damon. How to Rehearse a Play. Milton Park, Abingdon. Taylor & Francis. July 28, 2020.

Logan, John. *Red.* Dramatist. New York, New York. Dramatists Play Service, Inc. April 27, 2011.

Mamet, David. *Oleanna*. New York, New York. Vintage. May 4, 1993.

McQuiston, John. *Always We Begin Again: The Benedictine Way of Living*. Harrisburg, Pennsylvania. Morehouse Publishing. April 1, 1996.

Mitchell, Katie. *The Director's Craft: A Handbook for the Theatre*. New York, New York. Routledge. October 5, 2008.

Nottage, Lynn. *Sweat*. New York, New York. Theatre Communications Group. June 13, 2017.

Nozicka, Paloma. "Enough to Let the Light In". September 28, 2022. New Play Exchange.

Oliver, Mary. *Red Bird: Poems*. Boston, Massachusetts. Beacon Press. April 1, 2009.

Pinter, Harold. *Old Times*. New York, New York. Grove Press. January 13, 1994.

Rebeck, Theresa. *Mauritius*. New York, New York. Concord Theatricals. March 12, 2009.

Reza, Yasmina. *Art*. New York, New York. Farrar, Straus and Giroux. March 6, 1997.

Ruhl, Sarah. *100 Essays I Don't Have Time to Write: On Umbrellas and Sword Fights, Parades and Dogs, Fire Alarms, Children, and Theater*. New York, New York. Farrar, Straus and Giroux. Sept, 15 2015.

Rylance, Mark. "You have to move into the chaos." Interview by Rachel Cooke. *The Guardian*, Jul. 2013

Viorst, Judith. *Alexander and the Terrible, Horrible, No Good, Very Bad Day*. New York, New York. Simon & Schuster. January 7, 2014.

Weil, Simone. *First and Last Notebooks: Supernatural Knowledge*. Eugene, Oregon. Wipf and Stock. January 1, 1667.

Willingham, Emily. "People Have Been Having Less Sex—whether They're Teenagers or 40-Somethings". Scientific American. January 3, 2022.

Acknowledgments

It takes a lot of ego to write a book. One which I don't always possess. I remember teaching Peter Brook's *The Empty Space* in a collaboration class at DePaul University.

One of my students, Coral Gable, declared: Wow, this guy is an asshole. He's so sure of himself.

Me: Well, Coral, no one wants to read a book full of "maybes", "I think", and "I guess so." It requires a certain amount of fortitude in your convictions to write all these things down.

None of these words would have been written without my huge, vibrant, supportive community.

Addie Gorlin, Kate Bergstrom and Ashley Teague for our weekly sessions during the pandemic and helping me keep this project alive. Our Lady Director Batphone Text Chat has inspired a lot of this book.

Lukas Brasher-Fons for early feedback and the most genuine discerning eye. Sharifa Yazmeen for infinite encouragement and bibliography organizing.

All my students- past, present, and future- you are my "why" for so much of what I do in this life.

My art partners- Eleanor Burgess, Tony Crane, Jessiee Datino, Behzad Dabu, Sandra Delgado, Hari Dhillon, Ellen Fairey, Jessie Fisher, Kate

Fry, Kirsten Greenidge, Erik Hellman, Nathan "Buddy" Hosner, Gloria Calderón Kellett, Shane Kenyon, Mark Montgomery, Deanna Myers, Caroline Neff, Patrick Sabongui, Cassidy Slaughter-Mason, Alix Sobler, Nisi Sturgis, Bernie White, and so many more- you necessitate my articulation and specificity while inspiring me with your artistry every day.

My collaborators in design- Cameron Anderson, Brian Sidney Bembridge, Jill DuBoff, Sarita Fellows, M.L. Geiger, Heather Gilbert, Jack Magaw, Frank Oliva, Joanna Lynne Staub, Misha Fiksel, D.M. Wood and so many more- you push me to think and speak in new ways and open my mind to possibilities I never knew existed.

My fellow directors- Lili-Anne Brown, Curt Columbus, Lyndsay Allyn Cox, Rachel Dart, Pascale Florestal, Keira Fromm, Faith Hart, Damon Kiely, Marti Lyons, Megan Sandberg-Zakian, Joanie Schultz, Sharifa Yasmin and Pirronne Yousefzadeh- our conversations, our support groups, our exchanged life and directing hacks have such a profound influence on how I walk through both my professional and personal spaces.

Martha Lavey, Mary Ann Thebus and Lisa Banes for believing in me even when I didn't, for pushing me when I didn't want to be pushed, and for modeling the myriad ways to be women and artists and leaders.

PS Masri for giving me a new lease on life. For creating space, actual space, in which I could write. For being both a bully and a cheerleader all at once. For inspiring me daily with your advocacy, your artistry, and your integrity. It is in your gaze that I am invincible.

Mom and Dad for giving me boundaries when I needed them and freedom when I needed it more. I could write a whole other book about your advice and what I've gleaned from 51 years of being your child.

Noah and Delaney, when I first heard José Rivera say "Make babies and make art for them." I understood my purpose. Every breath I take is an attempt to make the world make sense for you, not to protect you from it, but to prepare you for it. The only secrets I've got are inside these pages.